I0794803

PARADES OF THE WEHRMACHT
Berlin 1934-1940

Heroes' Memorial Day in Berlin, 1935. The flags of the old Army before decoration with the Cross of Honor at the barrack grounds of the "Command of the Guard Troops."

Horst Scheibert

PARADES OF THE WEHRMACHT

Berlin 1934-1940

A guard company marches through the Brandenburg Gate in 1934.

Schiffer Military History
Atglen, PA

Cover Photo
Birthday Parade, 1938, before the University. The Panzerkampfwagen II. At left a Panzer IIb with the standard (behind the commander) of a unit of Panzer Regiment 5 from Wünsdorf, south of Berlin. The standard bears the colors rose, black and rose. In the upper rose, the number 5 can be seen. The tank at the right front in a IIc, as is the one following it. The standard-bearer with the standard is in the latter tank.

Back Cover
Paratroopers parade before Hitler on his birthday in 1939, on the East-West Axis in Berlin.

SOURCES
Bundesarchiv
Hans-Peter Dabrowski Archives
Horst Scheibert Archives
Podzun-Pallas Archives

Translated from the German by Dr. Edward Force.

This book was originally published under the title,
Paraden der Wehrmacht, Berlin 1934-1940,
by Podzun-Pallas Verlag.

Copyright © 1997 by Schiffer Publishing Ltd.
Library of Congress Catalog Number: 96-70670.

All rights reserved. No part of this work may be reproduced or used in any forms or by any means – graphic, electronic or mechanical, including photocopying or information storage and retrieval systems – without written permission from the copyright holder.

Printed in China.
ISBN: 0-7643-0231-0

We are interested in hearing from authors with book ideas on related topics.

Published by Schiffer Publishing Ltd.
77 Lower Valley Road
Atglen, PA 19310
Phone: (610) 593-1777
FAX: (610) 593-2002
Please write for a free catalog.
This book may be purchased from the publisher.
Please include $2.95 postage.
Try your bookstore first.

CONTENTS

An honor company marches to receive the new Soviet ambassador, Berlin 1939.

FOREWORD

We had some hesitation about producing a pictorial volume showing parades of the Wehrmacht, until we saw that in those days the participating troop units presented their equipment, weapons and uniforms with a high polish, and the pictures of them were technically excellent.

Since the parades took place, for the most part, in the prewar years during the building up of the Wehrmacht, the pictures show many early types of equipment and uniforms of which there are otherwise very few photographs. This is especially true of the Panzer troops.

Paratroops march past the reviewing stand in Hitler's birthday parade on the East-West Axis in Berlin, 1939.

PARADES IN BERLIN

By parades we mean the gathering or marching of troops, along with the playing of marching music, past high-ranking officers, chiefs of state, usually on the occasion of memorial days, to honor high-ranking visitors, or as the conclusion of inspections and major drills — the latter were also called field parades. In contrast to the first, which were specially made with highly polished uniforms, weapons and vehicles, the latter were made in field outfits.

In Berlin, as the capital city of the Reich, only the first type of parades by the Reichswehr, and particularly the Wehrmacht, took place. The occasions were (among others):

Heroes' Memorial Days
Hitler's Birthdays, and
to honor foreign guests,

1934

An honor guard marches by the war memorial on its way to lay a wreath on the occasion of a visit by the chief of the Hungarian military command, General Karpathy, in 1934. Karpathy and his party are wearing steel helmets.

1934: A Reichswehr honor guard marches past the war memorial during the Brzezany Celebration. The flag bearers carry the flags of the regiments involved in the breakthrough. On August 28, 1915, a great break through the Russian front took place near Tarnopol, in Galicia.

The Guard Troop Command, gathered on the Moabit Drill Field on February 16, 1934, is reviewed by the new Chief of Army Operations, General of the Artillery von Fritsch (with cap). Behind him (right) is the regimental commander, Oberst von Keiser, at left are the Commandant of Berlin, General Schaumburg, and the Defense District Commander, General von Witzleben.

Reviewing the Guard of Honor gathered before the War Memorial in 1934 is the Chief of Army Operations, General of the Artillery von Fritsch. The occasion was the 20th anniversary of the Battle of Tannenberg in East Prussia. Next to General von Fritsch are Generals (right to left) bon Rundstedt and von Witzleben.

1934: A Chinese study commission, with the Vice-Minister of Transport and several high Chinese officials, review the guard of honor after laying a wreath at the War Memorial.

1934: A guard of honor marches past after the laying of a wreath by Finnish Major General Heinrichs in memory of a German U-boat that was sunk in battle off Finland in World War I. The honor guard wears black armbands.

Pour-le-merite Knights' Day, 1935: The honor guard of the Reichsheer is being inspected by Field Marshal von Mackensen in front of the War Memorial.

While usually only the guard or training battalions, individually or together (Army, Navy and Luftwaffe) were involved in the last, parades for Hitler's birthday, since he was then the head of state, were typified by particularly great extent and splendor. Here, as a matter of course, whole troop units of all branches of the Wehrmacht took part, with the Army units also presenting arms. The streets on the parade routes — usually "Unter den Linden", "Charlottenburger Chaussee" or "Ost-West-Achse" — and public squares were also decorated with pennants and many flags, plus large grandstands for guests and spectators.

All parades were naturally also a demonstration of power, and media of all kinds (newspapers, radio and film, newsreels in the cinemas) reported in depth to give the entire Reich and other countries information about the events, complete with pictures and propaganda.

Along with the Guard Battalion ("Wachregiment Berlin" as of 1937), which marched daily to and from its guard duties (Brandenburg Gate, Wache, etc.) or took part in parades along with troop units of the Navy and Luftwaffe for visits of foreign guests, other troop units from the Berlin area also turned out for important occasions. Usually there were Infantry Regiment 9 (Potsdam) and parts of the 3rd Panzer Division (with its staff in Berlin), but as of 1938, formerly Austrian troop units or special groups such as cavalry, paratroops and others were also called in. Usually there were also the instructional battalions (or regiments) of the service arms, and for the Luftwaffe, troop units of the Luftwaffe "Regiment General Göring" (RGG), plus the Naval Officers' Training Unit for the Navy.

Marching out on Heroes' Memorial Day in March 1935. With the flags of the old regiments, the soldiers march through the Brandenburg Gate.

1935

Heroes' Memorial Day 1935: Firing a salute in the Berlin Lustgarten during the attachments of the Cross of Honor to the traditional flags.

Heroes' Memorial Day 1935: Marching with the traditional flags from the Lustgarten to the War Memorial (Unter den linden) after attachment of the Crosses of Honor.

Announcement of military freedom in the Berlin Lustgarten in 1935.

Below: A postcard of 1935.

1936

1936: The Guard Company of the "Wachtruppe Berlin" drills in its barracks grounds before marching to the War Memorial, practicing the presenting of arms.

Above and below: Honor units of the three arms of the Wehrmacht march past Hitler at the War Memorial on Heroes' Memorial Day, March 1936. Here we see the units of the Army that carry the old flags.

Birthday Parade, 1936: View of the Charlottenburger Chaussee from the Brandenburg Gate. Panzerwagen IA — also called "Krupp-Sport" — can be seen. This was the first armored vehicle that reached the troops in large numbers, beginning in 1935.

Before Hitler's birthday parade in 1936, which took place on the Charlottenburger Chaussee, Hitler (left front in the first car) reviews the assembled troops. The Panzerwagen I to be seen here — originally planned only as a training tank — still saw action in the first years of the war.

IIA-19357
IIA-19356

Birthday Parade, 1936: Armored scout cars (4- and 6-wheel) and motorized artillery (right) wait in the lustgarten for the command to march in the parade.

For the same parade, there have assembled in the Lustgarten in front of the Castle: Motorized infantry in the center, motorized rifle units at right, and antitank forces at left, with their 3.7 cm antitank guns (Pak).

The Panzer troops on parade. Above, on Unter den Linden, below before Hitler (with the commanders of the three Wehrmacht arms behind him). These are Panzerwagen IA. They are recognizable by the four road wheels (the 1B had five) and the exhaust pipes on the track aprons. The 1B had them on the rear. The second tank in the right column above is a small Command Car 1A with fixed turret —here in very unusual form, without a machine gun.

The 1936 Birthday Parade on the Charlottenburger Chaussee. An infantry unit marches past.

Infantry regiments prepare to receive new flags on the barrack grounds of the "Guard Regiment Berlin" on Rathenower Strasse.

Parade of the Naval Unteroffizier Training Unit before Field Marshal von Blomberg, honoring his forty years in service.

1937

In the same parade, a guard company of the "Regiment General Göring" (RGG) marches by.

Heroes' Memorial Day, 1937: The flag company marches onto the Pariser Platz.

April 19, 1937, Wilhelmsplatz in Berlin: Ninety new flags are turned over to the three Wehrmacht branches by Hitler.

The great parade on Hitler's birthday in 1937, on the Charlottenburger Chaussee. An infantry unit marches past the Technische Hochschule, with the Music Corps in the foreground.

Birthday Parade, 1937: Horsedrawn units of the infantry, with a heavy machine-gun company in the foreground. The old water-cooled machine guns can be seen.

Birthday Parade, 1937, on the Charlottenburger Chaussee. The 1st Naval Unteroffizier Training Unit marches by.

Birthday Parade, 1937, on the Charlottenburger Chaussee. Sections of the (Luftwaffe) "Regiment General Göring" (RGG) march by.

Birthday Parade, 1937, on the Charlottenburger Chaussee. Motorcycle riflemen on BMW R12 motorcycles.

Birthday Parade, 1937, on the Charlottenburger Chaussee. A Panzer troop unit, with a Panzerkampfwagen IB (foreground) and Panzerkampfwagen IA behind it.

Birthday Parade, 1937, on the Charlottenburger Chaussee. Once again we see the Naval Unteroffizier Training Unit.

The Italian Propaganda Minister is to lay a wreath at the War Memorial. The Italian guests wear black uniforms. The guard of honor marches past them.

The honor guard marches past after the laying of a wreath at the War Memorial by Field Marshal von Mackensen on the 224th birthday of Frederick the Great, under the auspices of the knights of the order of "Pour le merite", an order created by Frederick the Great.

1938

The 1938 Birthday Parade passes the University on Unter den Linden. A bicycle company of an infantry regiment is shown.

The 1938 Birthday Parade. An infantry regiment marches past the University. In the left foreground, the monument to Frederick the Great can be seen.

The 1938 Birthday Parade, with the head of an infantry regiment.

The 1938 Birthday Parade in front of the University, with the head of the (former) Linz House Regiment.

The 1938 Birthday Parade in front of the University. This unit was also part of the Austrian Army a short time ago.

The 1938 Birthday Parade in front of the University. A Panzer unit approaches. In front is a Panzerwagen III, Type A, with large road wheels, then a Panzerwagen IV Type A, recognizable by the cylindrical commander's cupola. In the left background is a Panzerwagen II.

The 1938 Birthday Parade in front of the University. Panzerkampfwagen IB.

The parade for the Hungarian Regent von Horthy on August 25, 1938. Grandstands in front of the Technische Hochschule, with the Hungarian coat of arms on the front of the building. In the foreground are two lFH 18 guns of a horsedrawn artillery battery.

The parade for the Hungarian Regent von Horthy falls in on August 25, 1938. In the right column are Panzer III tanks; beside them are Panzer II, with Panzer I far to the rear. The left column has vehicles of a rifle regiment, whose crews are lined up to the left of them. At the far left, in a column of cars, are Horthy and Hitler in the first car.

The parade for the Hungarian Regent von Horthy. Panzer IB in front, Panzer II in back.

November 13, 1938: After laying a wreath at the War Memorial in memory of the battle of Langemarck in November 1914, an honor guard of the Army marches past the Memorial.

The Grosse Wache marching by the War Memorial in Berlin in 1939.

1939

Heroes' Memorial Day, March 12, 1939. Both pictures show an honor battalion made up of men from the three services, marching past the War Memorial, lewd by (above) the flag company with the old flags. Hitler and the three commanders-in-chief review the troops.

Another view of the parade on Heroes' Memorial Day, 1939.

The Birthday Parade on the East-West-Axis. Above and below: the flag battalion marches by.

The 1939 Birthday Parade on the East-West-Axis. A motorcycle rifle battalion passes. Photographed from the Tiergarten Station.

The 1939 Birthday Parade on the East-West-Axis. This parade was the first in which the paratroops marched.

The 1939 Birthday Parade on the East-West-Axis. A Panzer regiment is passing by, with Panzer II in front and Panzer III in the background. In the first Panzer II stands the standard-bearer with the regimental standard.

The 1939 Birthday Parade on the East-West Axis. Panzer I and II carried on trucks and low loaders pass by. Only the Panzer units of the three light divisions carried their tanks thus, and it was given up before the war began.

These photos were also taken during the 1939 Birthday Parade on the East-West-Axis. Above, the Panzer units seen from another angle. The trucks with their low-loader trailers can be seen clearly. Below, a horsedrawn artillery unit with lFH 18 guns, and a band in the foreground.

The guard marches on Unter den Linden in 1939.

For the visit of the Prince Regent couple of Yugoslavia on June 2, 1939, a large Wehrmacht parade took place. Here a cavalry regiment marches past, with a trumpeter corps at right.

The visit of the Prince Regent couple of Yugoslavia on June 2, 1939. A horsedrawn artillery unit with lFH 18 guns marches by.

The visit of the Prince Regent couple of Yugoslavia on June 2, 1939. A motorized artillery battery with sFH 18 guns marches by.

Motorized and armored units fall in line on the East-West-Axis, in front of the Brandenburg Gate, for the visit of the Yugoslavian Prince Regent couple on June 2, 1939.

The paratroops march by.

The Berlin Guard Regiment marches on its barrack grounds (Rathenow Street) for its formal renaming as the "Grossdeutschland Regiment" (GD), June 14, 1939.

1940

Unter den Linden, 1940: a Brandenburg division returns home after the end of the campaign against France. Here the men are welcomed by the people of Berlin.

A Berlin troop unit is welcomed back at the Brandenburg Gate after the end of the French campaign.

AFTERWORD

When looking at the photos in this book, one may experience strong feelings. Over half of the soldiers seen here were soon dead or wounded in action, and the great majority of them surely died firmly believing they had served a good cause. Today, though, we know that they were sacrificed by a megalomaniacal dictator who started an unnecessary war and took it to criminal and inhuman extremes. What a crime against humanity, and what a misuse of the Wehrmacht! The past must surely be understood in terms of its times — but from it we can also learn lessons to apply to building a better future, which can be done without using parades as demonstrations of might and strength.